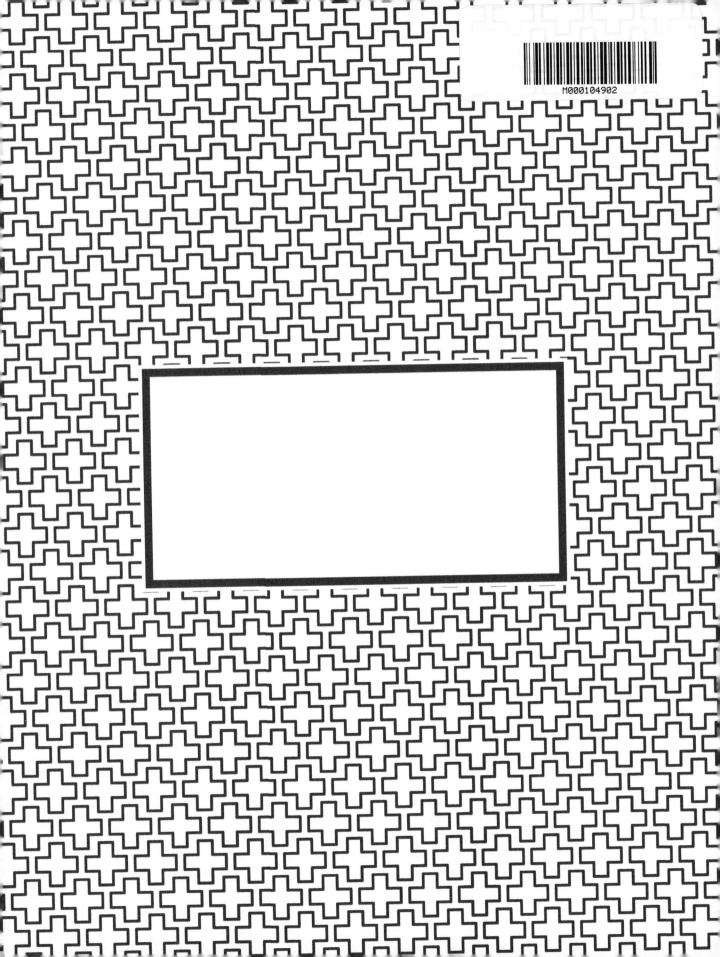

TODAY'S DATE:

TODAY'S VERSE: _____

_____
_____
_____
_____
_____
_____
_____
_____
_____
_____
_____
_____
_____

HOW IT APPLIES TO MY LIFE:

_____
_____
_____
_____
_____
_____
_____
_____
_____
_____
_____
_____
_____
_____

I'M PRAYING FOR: _____

_____
_____
_____
_____
_____
_____

I'M THANKFUL FOR: _____

_____
_____
_____
_____
_____

TODAY'S DATE:

TODAY'S VERSE: _____

_____
_____
_____
_____
_____
_____
_____
_____
_____
_____
_____
_____
_____

HOW IT APPLIES TO MY LIFE:

_____
_____
_____
_____
_____
_____
_____
_____
_____
_____
_____
_____
_____

I'M PRAYING FOR: _____

_____
_____
_____
_____
_____

I'M THANKFUL FOR: _____

_____
_____
_____
_____
_____

TODAY'S DATE:

TODAY'S VERSE: _____

_____
_____
_____
_____
_____
_____
_____
_____
_____
_____
_____
_____

HOW IT APPLIES TO MY LIFE:

_____
_____
_____
_____
_____
_____
_____
_____
_____
_____
_____
_____

I'M PRAYING FOR: _____

_____
_____
_____
_____
_____
_____

I'M THANKFUL FOR: _____

_____
_____
_____
_____
_____

TODAY'S DATE:

TODAY'S VERSE: _____

_____
_____
_____
_____
_____
_____
_____
_____
_____
_____
_____

HOW IT APPLIES TO MY LIFE:

_____
_____
_____
_____
_____
_____
_____
_____
_____
_____
_____
_____
_____
_____

I'M PRAYING FOR: _____

_____
_____
_____
_____
_____
_____

I'M THANKFUL FOR: _____

_____
_____
_____
_____
_____

TODAY'S DATE: _____

TODAY'S VERSE: _____
_____
_____
_____
_____
_____
_____
_____
_____
_____
_____
_____
_____
_____
_____
_____

HOW IT APPLIES TO MY LIFE:
_____
_____
_____
_____
_____
_____
_____
_____
_____
_____
_____
_____
_____
_____
_____
_____

I'M PRAYING FOR: _____
_____
_____
_____
_____
_____
_____

I'M THANKFUL FOR: _____
_____
_____
_____
_____
_____

TODAY'S DATE:

TODAY'S VERSE: _____

_____
_____
_____
_____
_____
_____
_____
_____
_____
_____
_____
_____
_____

HOW IT APPLIES TO MY LIFE:

_____
_____
_____
_____
_____
_____
_____
_____
_____
_____
_____
_____
_____
_____
_____

I'M PRAYING FOR: _____

_____
_____
_____
_____
_____

I'M THANKFUL FOR: _____

_____
_____
_____
_____
_____

TODAY'S DATE:

TODAY'S VERSE: _____

_____
_____
_____
_____
_____
_____
_____
_____
_____
_____
_____
_____

HOW IT APPLIES TO MY LIFE:

_____
_____
_____
_____
_____
_____
_____
_____
_____
_____
_____
_____
_____

I'M PRAYING FOR: _____

_____
_____
_____
_____
_____
_____

I'M THANKFUL FOR: _____

_____
_____
_____
_____
_____

TODAY'S DATE:

TODAY'S VERSE: _____

_____
_____
_____
_____
_____
_____
_____
_____
_____
_____
_____

HOW IT APPLIES TO MY LIFE:

_____
_____
_____
_____
_____
_____
_____
_____
_____
_____
_____
_____

I'M PRAYING FOR: _____

_____
_____
_____
_____
_____

I'M THANKFUL FOR: _____

_____
_____
_____
_____

TODAY'S DATE:

TODAY'S VERSE: _____

_____
_____
_____
_____
_____
_____
_____
_____
_____
_____
_____

HOW IT APPLIES TO MY LIFE:

_____
_____
_____
_____
_____
_____
_____
_____
_____
_____
_____
_____

I'M PRAYING FOR: _____

_____
_____
_____
_____
_____

I'M THANKFUL FOR: _____

_____
_____
_____
_____
_____

TODAY'S DATE:

TODAY'S VERSE: _____

_____
_____
_____
_____
_____
_____
_____
_____
_____
_____
_____
_____

HOW IT APPLIES TO MY LIFE:

_____
_____
_____
_____
_____
_____
_____
_____
_____
_____
_____
_____
_____
_____

I'M PRAYING FOR: _____

_____
_____
_____
_____

I'M THANKFUL FOR: _____

_____
_____
_____
_____

TODAY'S DATE:

TODAY'S VERSE: _____

_____
_____
_____
_____
_____
_____
_____
_____
_____
_____
_____
_____
_____

HOW IT APPLIES TO MY LIFE:

_____
_____
_____
_____
_____
_____
_____
_____
_____
_____
_____
_____
_____

I'M PRAYING FOR: _____

_____
_____
_____
_____
_____
_____

I'M THANKFUL FOR: _____

_____
_____
_____
_____
_____
_____

TODAY'S DATE:

TODAY'S VERSE: _____

HOW IT APPLIES TO MY LIFE:

I'M PRAYING FOR: _____

I'M THANKFUL FOR: _____

TODAY'S DATE:

TODAY'S VERSE: _____

_____
_____
_____
_____
_____
_____
_____
_____
_____
_____
_____
_____

HOW IT APPLIES TO MY LIFE:

_____
_____
_____
_____
_____
_____
_____
_____
_____
_____
_____
_____
_____
_____
_____

I'M PRAYING FOR: _____

_____
_____
_____
_____
_____

I'M THANKFUL FOR: _____

_____
_____
_____
_____

TODAY'S DATE:

TODAY'S VERSE: _____

_____
_____
_____
_____
_____
_____
_____
_____
_____
_____
_____
_____
_____

HOW IT APPLIES TO MY LIFE:

_____
_____
_____
_____
_____
_____
_____
_____
_____
_____
_____
_____
_____

I'M PRAYING FOR: _____

_____
_____
_____
_____

I'M THANKFUL FOR: _____

_____
_____
_____
_____

TODAY'S DATE:

TODAY'S VERSE: _____

_____
_____
_____
_____
_____
_____
_____
_____
_____
_____
_____
_____
_____

HOW IT APPLIES TO MY LIFE:

_____
_____
_____
_____
_____
_____
_____
_____
_____
_____
_____
_____
_____

I'M PRAYING FOR: _____

_____
_____
_____
_____
_____

I'M THANKFUL FOR: _____

_____
_____
_____
_____
_____

TODAY'S DATE:

TODAY'S VERSE: _____

_____
_____
_____
_____
_____
_____
_____
_____
_____
_____
_____
_____

HOW IT APPLIES TO MY LIFE:

_____
_____
_____
_____
_____
_____
_____
_____
_____
_____
_____
_____
_____

I'M PRAYING FOR: _____

_____
_____
_____
_____
_____
_____

I'M THANKFUL FOR: _____

_____
_____
_____
_____
_____

TODAY'S DATE:

TODAY'S VERSE: _____

_____
_____
_____
_____
_____
_____
_____
_____
_____
_____
_____
_____
_____
_____

HOW IT APPLIES TO MY LIFE:

_____
_____
_____
_____
_____
_____
_____
_____
_____
_____
_____
_____
_____
_____

I'M PRAYING FOR: _____

_____
_____
_____
_____
_____
_____

I'M THANKFUL FOR: _____

_____
_____
_____
_____
_____
_____

TODAY'S DATE:

TODAY'S VERSE: _____

_____
_____
_____
_____
_____
_____
_____
_____
_____
_____
_____
_____

HOW IT APPLIES TO MY LIFE:

_____
_____
_____
_____
_____
_____
_____
_____
_____
_____
_____
_____
_____

I'M PRAYING FOR: _____

_____
_____
_____
_____
_____
_____

I'M THANKFUL FOR: _____

_____
_____
_____
_____
_____
_____

TODAY'S DATE:

TODAY'S VERSE: _____

_____
_____
_____
_____
_____
_____
_____
_____
_____
_____
_____
_____

HOW IT APPLIES TO MY LIFE:

_____
_____
_____
_____
_____
_____
_____
_____
_____
_____
_____
_____
_____

I'M PRAYING FOR: _____

_____
_____
_____
_____
_____

I'M THANKFUL FOR: _____

_____
_____
_____
_____
_____

TODAY'S DATE:

TODAY'S VERSE: _____

_____
_____
_____
_____
_____
_____
_____
_____
_____
_____
_____

HOW IT APPLIES TO MY LIFE:

_____
_____
_____
_____
_____
_____
_____
_____
_____
_____
_____
_____
_____
_____

I'M PRAYING FOR: _____

_____
_____
_____
_____
_____
_____

I'M THANKFUL FOR: _____

_____
_____
_____
_____
_____
_____

TODAY'S DATE:

TODAY'S VERSE: _____
_____
_____
_____
_____
_____
_____
_____
_____
_____
_____
_____
_____
_____

HOW IT APPLIES TO MY LIFE:
_____
_____
_____
_____
_____
_____
_____
_____
_____
_____
_____
_____
_____

I'M PRAYING FOR: _____
_____
_____
_____
_____
_____
_____

I'M THANKFUL FOR: _____
_____
_____
_____
_____
_____

TODAY'S DATE:

TODAY'S VERSE: _____

_____
_____
_____
_____
_____
_____
_____
_____
_____
_____
_____

HOW IT APPLIES TO MY LIFE:

_____
_____
_____
_____
_____
_____
_____
_____
_____
_____
_____
_____
_____

I'M PRAYING FOR: _____

_____
_____
_____
_____
_____

I'M THANKFUL FOR: _____

_____
_____
_____
_____
_____

TODAY'S DATE:

TODAY'S VERSE: _____

_____
_____
_____
_____
_____
_____
_____
_____
_____
_____
_____
_____
_____

HOW IT APPLIES TO MY LIFE:

_____
_____
_____
_____
_____
_____
_____
_____
_____
_____
_____
_____

I'M PRAYING FOR: _____

_____
_____
_____
_____
_____

I'M THANKFUL FOR: _____

_____
_____
_____
_____
_____

TODAY'S DATE:

TODAY'S VERSE: _____

_____
_____
_____
_____
_____
_____
_____
_____
_____
_____
_____
_____

HOW IT APPLIES TO MY LIFE:

_____
_____
_____
_____
_____
_____
_____
_____
_____
_____
_____
_____
_____

I'M PRAYING FOR: _____

_____
_____
_____
_____
_____
_____

I'M THANKFUL FOR: _____

_____
_____
_____
_____
_____

TODAY'S DATE:

TODAY'S VERSE: _____

_____
_____
_____
_____
_____
_____
_____
_____
_____
_____
_____

HOW IT APPLIES TO MY LIFE:

_____
_____
_____
_____
_____
_____
_____
_____
_____
_____

I'M PRAYING FOR: _____

_____
_____
_____
_____

I'M THANKFUL FOR: _____

_____
_____
_____
_____

TODAY'S DATE:

TODAY'S VERSE: _____

HOW IT APPLIES TO MY LIFE:

I'M PRAYING FOR: _____

I'M THANKFUL FOR: _____

TODAY'S DATE:

TODAY'S VERSE: _____

_____
_____
_____
_____
_____
_____
_____
_____
_____
_____
_____
_____
_____
_____

HOW IT APPLIES TO MY LIFE:

_____
_____
_____
_____
_____
_____
_____
_____
_____
_____
_____
_____
_____
_____
_____

I'M PRAYING FOR: _____

_____
_____
_____
_____
_____
_____

I'M THANKFUL FOR: _____

_____
_____
_____
_____
_____
_____

TODAY'S DATE:

TODAY'S VERSE: _____

_____
_____
_____
_____
_____
_____
_____
_____
_____
_____
_____

HOW IT APPLIES TO MY LIFE:

_____
_____
_____
_____
_____
_____
_____
_____
_____
_____
_____

I'M PRAYING FOR: _____

_____
_____
_____
_____
_____

I'M THANKFUL FOR: _____

_____
_____
_____
_____

TODAY'S DATE: _____

TODAY'S VERSE: _____
_____
_____
_____
_____
_____
_____
_____
_____
_____
_____
_____
_____
_____

HOW IT APPLIES TO MY LIFE:
_____
_____
_____
_____
_____
_____
_____
_____
_____
_____
_____
_____
_____

I'M PRAYING FOR: _____
_____
_____
_____
_____
_____
_____

I'M THANKFUL FOR: _____
_____
_____
_____
_____
_____

TODAY'S DATE:

TODAY'S VERSE: _____

_____
_____
_____
_____
_____
_____
_____
_____
_____
_____
_____
_____
_____
_____

HOW IT APPLIES TO MY LIFE:

_____
_____
_____
_____
_____
_____
_____
_____
_____
_____
_____
_____
_____
_____

I'M PRAYING FOR: _____

_____
_____
_____
_____
_____
_____

I'M THANKFUL FOR: _____

_____
_____
_____
_____
_____
_____

TODAY'S DATE:

TODAY'S VERSE: _____

_____
_____
_____
_____
_____
_____
_____
_____
_____
_____
_____
_____

HOW IT APPLIES TO MY LIFE:

_____
_____
_____
_____
_____
_____
_____
_____
_____
_____
_____
_____
_____
_____
_____

I'M PRAYING FOR: _____

_____
_____
_____
_____
_____

I'M THANKFUL FOR: _____

_____
_____
_____
_____
_____

TODAY'S DATE:

TODAY'S VERSE: _____

HOW IT APPLIES TO MY LIFE:

I'M PRAYING FOR: _____

I'M THANKFUL FOR: _____

TODAY'S DATE:

TODAY'S VERSE: _____

_____
_____
_____
_____
_____
_____
_____
_____
_____
_____
_____

HOW IT APPLIES TO MY LIFE:

_____
_____
_____
_____
_____
_____
_____
_____
_____
_____
_____

I'M PRAYING FOR: _____

_____
_____
_____
_____
_____

I'M THANKFUL FOR: _____

_____
_____
_____
_____
_____

TODAY'S DATE:

TODAY'S VERSE: _____

_____
_____
_____
_____
_____
_____
_____
_____
_____
_____
_____
_____

HOW IT APPLIES TO MY LIFE:

_____
_____
_____
_____
_____
_____
_____
_____
_____
_____
_____
_____
_____

I'M PRAYING FOR: _____

_____
_____
_____
_____
_____

I'M THANKFUL FOR: _____

_____
_____
_____
_____
_____

TODAY'S DATE:

TODAY'S VERSE: _____

_____
_____
_____
_____
_____
_____
_____
_____
_____
_____
_____
_____
_____
_____
_____

HOW IT APPLIES TO MY LIFE:

_____
_____
_____
_____
_____
_____
_____
_____
_____
_____
_____
_____
_____

I'M PRAYING FOR: _____

_____
_____
_____
_____
_____
_____

I'M THANKFUL FOR: _____

_____
_____
_____
_____
_____

TODAY'S DATE:

TODAY'S VERSE: _____

_____
_____
_____
_____
_____
_____
_____
_____
_____
_____
_____
_____
_____

HOW IT APPLIES TO MY LIFE:

_____
_____
_____
_____
_____
_____
_____
_____
_____
_____
_____

I'M PRAYING FOR: _____

_____
_____
_____
_____
_____
_____

I'M THANKFUL FOR: _____

_____
_____
_____
_____
_____

TODAY'S DATE:

TODAY'S VERSE: _____

_____
_____
_____
_____
_____
_____
_____
_____
_____
_____
_____
_____
_____

HOW IT APPLIES TO MY LIFE:

_____
_____
_____
_____
_____
_____
_____
_____
_____
_____
_____
_____

I'M PRAYING FOR: _____

_____
_____
_____
_____
_____
_____

I'M THANKFUL FOR: _____

_____
_____
_____
_____
_____

TODAY'S DATE:

TODAY'S VERSE: _____

HOW IT APPLIES TO MY LIFE:

I'M PRAYING FOR: _____

I'M THANKFUL FOR: _____

TODAY'S DATE:

TODAY'S VERSE: _____
_____
_____
_____
_____
_____
_____
_____
_____
_____
_____
_____
_____
_____
_____
_____

HOW IT APPLIES TO MY LIFE:
_____
_____
_____
_____
_____
_____
_____
_____
_____
_____
_____
_____
_____
_____
_____
_____

I'M PRAYING FOR: _____
_____
_____
_____
_____
_____

I'M THANKFUL FOR: _____
_____
_____
_____
_____

TODAY'S DATE:

TODAY'S VERSE: _____

_____
_____
_____
_____
_____
_____
_____
_____
_____
_____
_____
_____

HOW IT APPLIES TO MY LIFE:

_____
_____
_____
_____
_____
_____
_____
_____
_____
_____
_____
_____
_____
_____

I'M PRAYING FOR: _____

_____
_____
_____
_____
_____
_____

I'M THANKFUL FOR: _____

_____
_____
_____
_____
_____

TODAY'S DATE:

TODAY'S VERSE: _____

_____
_____
_____
_____
_____
_____
_____
_____
_____
_____
_____
_____

HOW IT APPLIES TO MY LIFE:

_____
_____
_____
_____
_____
_____
_____
_____
_____
_____
_____
_____

I'M PRAYING FOR: _____

_____
_____
_____
_____
_____

I'M THANKFUL FOR: _____

_____
_____
_____
_____
_____

TODAY'S DATE:

TODAY'S VERSE: _____

_____
_____
_____
_____
_____
_____
_____
_____
_____
_____
_____
_____

HOW IT APPLIES TO MY LIFE:

_____
_____
_____
_____
_____
_____
_____
_____
_____
_____
_____
_____
_____
_____

I'M PRAYING FOR: _____

_____
_____
_____
_____
_____

I'M THANKFUL FOR: _____

_____
_____
_____
_____
_____
_____

TODAY'S DATE:

TODAY'S VERSE: _____

_____
_____
_____
_____
_____
_____
_____
_____
_____
_____
_____
_____
_____

HOW IT APPLIES TO MY LIFE:

_____
_____
_____
_____
_____
_____
_____
_____
_____
_____
_____
_____

I'M PRAYING FOR: _____

_____
_____
_____
_____
_____

I'M THANKFUL FOR: _____

_____
_____
_____
_____
_____

TODAY'S DATE:

TODAY'S VERSE: _____

_____
_____
_____
_____
_____
_____
_____
_____
_____
_____
_____
_____

HOW IT APPLIES TO MY LIFE:

_____
_____
_____
_____
_____
_____
_____
_____
_____
_____
_____
_____
_____
_____

I'M PRAYING FOR: _____

_____
_____
_____
_____
_____

I'M THANKFUL FOR: _____

_____
_____
_____
_____
_____

TODAY'S DATE:

TODAY'S VERSE: _____

_____
_____
_____
_____
_____
_____
_____
_____
_____
_____
_____
_____
_____

HOW IT APPLIES TO MY LIFE:

_____
_____
_____
_____
_____
_____
_____
_____
_____
_____
_____
_____
_____
_____

I'M PRAYING FOR: _____

_____
_____
_____
_____
_____
_____

I'M THANKFUL FOR: _____

_____
_____
_____
_____
_____

TODAY'S DATE:

TODAY'S VERSE: _____

_____
_____
_____
_____
_____
_____
_____
_____
_____
_____
_____
_____
_____

HOW IT APPLIES TO MY LIFE:

_____
_____
_____
_____
_____
_____
_____
_____
_____
_____
_____
_____
_____
_____
_____

I'M PRAYING FOR: _____

_____
_____
_____
_____
_____

I'M THANKFUL FOR: _____

_____
_____
_____
_____
_____

TODAY'S DATE:

TODAY'S VERSE: _____

_____
_____
_____
_____
_____
_____
_____
_____
_____
_____
_____
_____
_____
_____

HOW IT APPLIES TO MY LIFE:

_____
_____
_____
_____
_____
_____
_____
_____
_____
_____
_____
_____
_____
_____

I'M PRAYING FOR: _____

_____
_____
_____
_____
_____

I'M THANKFUL FOR: _____

_____
_____
_____
_____
_____

TODAY'S DATE:

TODAY'S VERSE: _____

_____
_____
_____
_____
_____
_____
_____
_____
_____
_____
_____
_____

HOW IT APPLIES TO MY LIFE:

_____
_____
_____
_____
_____
_____
_____
_____
_____
_____
_____
_____
_____
_____

I'M PRAYING FOR: _____

_____
_____
_____
_____
_____
_____

I'M THANKFUL FOR: _____

_____
_____
_____
_____
_____

TODAY'S DATE:

TODAY'S VERSE: _____

_____
_____
_____
_____
_____
_____
_____
_____
_____
_____
_____
_____

HOW IT APPLIES TO MY LIFE:

_____
_____
_____
_____
_____
_____
_____
_____
_____
_____
_____

I'M PRAYING FOR: _____

_____
_____
_____
_____
_____

I'M THANKFUL FOR: _____

_____
_____
_____
_____
_____

TODAY'S DATE:

TODAY'S VERSE: _____

_____
_____
_____
_____
_____
_____
_____
_____
_____
_____
_____
_____
_____
_____

HOW IT APPLIES TO MY LIFE:

_____
_____
_____
_____
_____
_____
_____
_____
_____
_____
_____
_____
_____
_____
_____
_____
_____

I'M PRAYING FOR: _____

_____
_____
_____
_____
_____
_____

I'M THANKFUL FOR: _____

_____
_____
_____
_____
_____
_____

TODAY'S DATE:

TODAY'S VERSE: _____

_____
_____
_____
_____
_____
_____
_____
_____
_____
_____
_____
_____
_____

HOW IT APPLIES TO MY LIFE:

_____
_____
_____
_____
_____
_____
_____
_____
_____
_____
_____
_____
_____

I'M PRAYING FOR: _____

_____
_____
_____
_____
_____

I'M THANKFUL FOR: _____

_____
_____
_____
_____
_____

TODAY'S DATE:

TODAY'S VERSE: _____

_____
_____
_____
_____
_____
_____
_____
_____
_____
_____
_____
_____
_____
_____

HOW IT APPLIES TO MY LIFE:

_____
_____
_____
_____
_____
_____
_____
_____
_____
_____
_____
_____
_____
_____
_____
_____

I'M PRAYING FOR: _____

_____
_____
_____
_____
_____
_____

I'M THANKFUL FOR: _____

_____
_____
_____
_____
_____

TODAY'S DATE:

TODAY'S VERSE: _____

_____
_____
_____
_____
_____
_____
_____
_____
_____
_____
_____
_____
_____
_____
_____
_____

HOW IT APPLIES TO MY LIFE:

_____
_____
_____
_____
_____
_____
_____
_____
_____
_____
_____
_____
_____
_____
_____

I'M PRAYING FOR: _____

_____
_____
_____
_____
_____
_____

I'M THANKFUL FOR: _____

_____
_____
_____
_____
_____

TODAY'S DATE:

TODAY'S VERSE: _____

_____
_____
_____
_____
_____
_____
_____
_____
_____
_____
_____
_____
_____
_____

HOW IT APPLIES TO MY LIFE:

_____
_____
_____
_____
_____
_____
_____
_____
_____
_____
_____
_____
_____
_____
_____
_____
_____

I'M PRAYING FOR: _____

_____
_____
_____
_____
_____

I'M THANKFUL FOR: _____

_____
_____
_____
_____
_____

TODAY'S DATE:

TODAY'S VERSE: _____

_____
_____
_____
_____
_____
_____
_____
_____
_____
_____
_____
_____

HOW IT APPLIES TO MY LIFE:

_____
_____
_____
_____
_____
_____
_____
_____
_____
_____
_____

I'M PRAYING FOR: _____

_____
_____
_____
_____
_____

I'M THANKFUL FOR: _____

_____
_____
_____
_____
_____

TODAY'S DATE:

TODAY'S VERSE: _____

_____
_____
_____
_____
_____
_____
_____
_____
_____
_____
_____
_____

HOW IT APPLIES TO MY LIFE:

_____
_____
_____
_____
_____
_____
_____
_____
_____
_____
_____
_____
_____

I'M PRAYING FOR: _____

_____
_____
_____
_____
_____
_____

I'M THANKFUL FOR: _____

_____
_____
_____
_____
_____

TODAY'S DATE:

TODAY'S VERSE: _____

_____
_____
_____
_____
_____
_____
_____
_____
_____
_____
_____
_____
_____

HOW IT APPLIES TO MY LIFE:

_____
_____
_____
_____
_____
_____
_____
_____
_____
_____
_____
_____
_____
_____

I'M PRAYING FOR: _____

_____
_____
_____
_____
_____

I'M THANKFUL FOR: _____

_____
_____
_____
_____
_____

TODAY'S DATE:

TODAY'S VERSE: _____

_____
_____
_____
_____
_____
_____
_____
_____
_____
_____
_____
_____
_____

HOW IT APPLIES TO MY LIFE:

_____
_____
_____
_____
_____
_____
_____
_____
_____
_____
_____
_____
_____

I'M PRAYING FOR: _____

_____
_____
_____
_____
_____

I'M THANKFUL FOR: _____

_____
_____
_____
_____
_____
_____

TODAY'S DATE:

TODAY'S VERSE: _____

_____
_____
_____
_____
_____
_____
_____
_____
_____
_____
_____
_____
_____
_____

HOW IT APPLIES TO MY LIFE:

_____
_____
_____
_____
_____
_____
_____
_____
_____
_____
_____
_____
_____
_____

I'M PRAYING FOR: _____

_____
_____
_____
_____
_____
_____

I'M THANKFUL FOR: _____

_____
_____
_____
_____
_____
_____
_____

TODAY'S DATE:

TODAY'S VERSE: _____

_____
_____
_____
_____
_____
_____
_____
_____
_____
_____
_____
_____

HOW IT APPLIES TO MY LIFE:

_____
_____
_____
_____
_____
_____
_____
_____
_____
_____
_____
_____
_____
_____

I'M PRAYING FOR: _____

_____
_____
_____
_____
_____
_____

I'M THANKFUL FOR: _____

_____
_____
_____
_____
_____

TODAY'S DATE:

TODAY'S VERSE: _____

_____
_____
_____
_____
_____
_____
_____
_____
_____
_____
_____
_____
_____
_____
_____

HOW IT APPLIES TO MY LIFE:

_____
_____
_____
_____
_____
_____
_____
_____
_____
_____
_____
_____
_____
_____
_____

I'M PRAYING FOR: _____

_____
_____
_____
_____
_____

I'M THANKFUL FOR: _____

_____
_____
_____
_____
_____

TODAY'S DATE:

TODAY'S VERSE: _____

_____
_____
_____
_____
_____
_____
_____
_____
_____
_____
_____
_____

HOW IT APPLIES TO MY LIFE:

_____
_____
_____
_____
_____
_____
_____
_____
_____
_____
_____
_____
_____

I'M PRAYING FOR: _____

_____
_____
_____
_____
_____

I'M THANKFUL FOR: _____

_____
_____
_____
_____
_____
_____

TODAY'S DATE:

TODAY'S VERSE: _____

_____
_____
_____
_____
_____
_____
_____
_____
_____
_____
_____
_____
_____

HOW IT APPLIES TO MY LIFE:

_____
_____
_____
_____
_____
_____
_____
_____
_____
_____
_____
_____
_____

I'M PRAYING FOR: _____

_____
_____
_____
_____
_____

I'M THANKFUL FOR: _____

_____
_____
_____
_____
_____

TODAY'S DATE:

TODAY'S VERSE: _____

_____
_____
_____
_____
_____
_____
_____
_____
_____
_____
_____
_____

HOW IT APPLIES TO MY LIFE:

_____
_____
_____
_____
_____
_____
_____
_____
_____
_____
_____
_____
_____
_____

I'M PRAYING FOR: _____

_____
_____
_____
_____
_____
_____

I'M THANKFUL FOR: _____

_____
_____
_____
_____
_____

TODAY'S DATE: _____

TODAY'S VERSE: _____
_____
_____
_____
_____
_____
_____
_____
_____
_____
_____
_____
_____
_____

HOW IT APPLIES TO MY LIFE:
_____
_____
_____
_____
_____
_____
_____
_____
_____
_____
_____
_____
_____
_____

I'M PRAYING FOR: _____
_____
_____
_____
_____
_____
_____

I'M THANKFUL FOR: _____
_____
_____
_____
_____
_____

TODAY'S DATE:

TODAY'S VERSE: _____

_____
_____
_____
_____
_____
_____
_____
_____
_____
_____
_____
_____
_____

HOW IT APPLIES TO MY LIFE:

_____
_____
_____
_____
_____
_____
_____
_____
_____
_____
_____
_____
_____
_____
_____
_____

I'M PRAYING FOR: _____

_____
_____
_____
_____
_____
_____

I'M THANKFUL FOR: _____

_____
_____
_____
_____
_____
_____

TODAY'S DATE:

TODAY'S VERSE: _____
_____
_____
_____
_____
_____
_____
_____
_____
_____
_____
_____
_____

HOW IT APPLIES TO MY LIFE:
_____
_____
_____
_____
_____
_____
_____
_____
_____
_____
_____

I'M PRAYING FOR: _____
_____
_____
_____
_____
_____
_____

I'M THANKFUL FOR: _____
_____
_____
_____
_____
_____

TODAY'S DATE:

TODAY'S VERSE: _____

_____
_____
_____
_____
_____
_____
_____
_____
_____
_____
_____

HOW IT APPLIES TO MY LIFE:

_____
_____
_____
_____
_____
_____
_____
_____
_____
_____
_____
_____

I'M PRAYING FOR: _____

_____
_____
_____
_____
_____

I'M THANKFUL FOR: _____

_____
_____
_____
_____
_____

TODAY'S DATE:

TODAY'S VERSE: _____

_____
_____
_____
_____
_____
_____
_____
_____
_____
_____
_____
_____

HOW IT APPLIES TO MY LIFE:

_____
_____
_____
_____
_____
_____
_____
_____
_____
_____
_____
_____
_____

I'M PRAYING FOR: _____

_____
_____
_____
_____
_____
_____

I'M THANKFUL FOR: _____

_____
_____
_____
_____
_____

TODAY'S DATE:

TODAY'S VERSE: _____

_____
_____
_____
_____
_____
_____
_____
_____
_____
_____

HOW IT APPLIES TO MY LIFE:

_____
_____
_____
_____
_____
_____
_____
_____
_____
_____
_____
_____
_____

I'M PRAYING FOR: _____

_____
_____
_____
_____
_____
_____

I'M THANKFUL FOR: _____

_____
_____
_____
_____
_____

TODAY'S DATE:

TODAY'S VERSE: _____

_____
_____
_____
_____
_____
_____
_____
_____
_____
_____
_____
_____
_____

HOW IT APPLIES TO MY LIFE:

_____
_____
_____
_____
_____
_____
_____
_____
_____
_____
_____

I'M PRAYING FOR: _____

_____
_____
_____
_____
_____
_____

I'M THANKFUL FOR: _____

_____
_____
_____
_____
_____

TODAY'S DATE:

TODAY'S VERSE: _____

_____
_____
_____
_____
_____
_____
_____
_____
_____
_____
_____
_____
_____

HOW IT APPLIES TO MY LIFE:

_____
_____
_____
_____
_____
_____
_____
_____
_____
_____
_____
_____
_____
_____

I'M PRAYING FOR: _____

_____
_____
_____
_____
_____
_____

I'M THANKFUL FOR: _____

_____
_____
_____
_____
_____

TODAY'S DATE:

TODAY'S VERSE: _____

_____
_____
_____
_____
_____
_____
_____
_____
_____
_____
_____
_____

HOW IT APPLIES TO MY LIFE:

_____
_____
_____
_____
_____
_____
_____
_____
_____
_____
_____
_____

I'M PRAYING FOR: _____

_____
_____
_____
_____
_____

I'M THANKFUL FOR: _____

_____
_____
_____
_____
_____

TODAY'S DATE:

TODAY'S VERSE: _____

_____
_____
_____
_____
_____
_____
_____
_____
_____
_____
_____
_____

HOW IT APPLIES TO MY LIFE:

_____
_____
_____
_____
_____
_____
_____
_____
_____
_____
_____
_____
_____
_____

I'M PRAYING FOR: _____

_____
_____
_____
_____
_____

I'M THANKFUL FOR: _____

_____
_____
_____
_____
_____

TODAY'S DATE:

TODAY'S VERSE: _____

_____
_____
_____
_____
_____
_____
_____
_____
_____
_____
_____
_____

HOW IT APPLIES TO MY LIFE:

_____
_____
_____
_____
_____
_____
_____
_____
_____
_____
_____
_____

I'M PRAYING FOR: _____

_____
_____
_____
_____
_____

I'M THANKFUL FOR: _____

_____
_____
_____
_____
_____

TODAY'S DATE:

TODAY'S VERSE: _____

_____
_____
_____
_____
_____
_____
_____
_____
_____
_____
_____
_____
_____

HOW IT APPLIES TO MY LIFE:

_____
_____
_____
_____
_____
_____
_____
_____
_____
_____
_____
_____
_____
_____
_____
_____

I'M PRAYING FOR: _____

_____
_____
_____
_____
_____
_____

I'M THANKFUL FOR: _____

_____
_____
_____
_____
_____

TODAY'S DATE:

TODAY'S VERSE: _____

_____
_____
_____
_____
_____
_____
_____
_____
_____
_____
_____
_____
_____
_____
_____

HOW IT APPLIES TO MY LIFE:

_____
_____
_____
_____
_____
_____
_____
_____
_____
_____
_____
_____
_____

I'M PRAYING FOR: _____

_____
_____
_____
_____
_____
_____

I'M THANKFUL FOR: _____

_____
_____
_____
_____
_____
_____

TODAY'S DATE:

TODAY'S VERSE: _____

HOW IT APPLIES TO MY LIFE:

I'M PRAYING FOR: _____

I'M THANKFUL FOR: _____

TODAY'S DATE:

TODAY'S VERSE: _____

_____
_____
_____
_____
_____
_____
_____
_____
_____
_____
_____
_____
_____

HOW IT APPLIES TO MY LIFE:

_____
_____
_____
_____
_____
_____
_____
_____
_____
_____
_____

I'M PRAYING FOR: _____

_____
_____
_____
_____
_____

I'M THANKFUL FOR: _____

_____
_____
_____
_____
_____

TODAY'S DATE:

TODAY'S VERSE: _____

_____
_____
_____
_____
_____
_____
_____
_____
_____
_____
_____
_____

HOW IT APPLIES TO MY LIFE:

_____
_____
_____
_____
_____
_____
_____
_____
_____
_____
_____
_____
_____

I'M PRAYING FOR: _____

_____
_____
_____
_____
_____

I'M THANKFUL FOR: _____

_____
_____
_____
_____
_____

TODAY'S DATE:

TODAY'S VERSE: _____

_____
_____
_____
_____
_____
_____
_____
_____
_____
_____
_____
_____
_____
_____

HOW IT APPLIES TO MY LIFE:

_____
_____
_____
_____
_____
_____
_____
_____
_____
_____
_____
_____
_____

I'M PRAYING FOR: _____

_____
_____
_____
_____
_____

I'M THANKFUL FOR: _____

_____
_____
_____
_____
_____

TODAY'S DATE:

TODAY'S VERSE: _____

_____
_____
_____
_____
_____
_____
_____
_____
_____
_____
_____
_____

HOW IT APPLIES TO MY LIFE:

_____
_____
_____
_____
_____
_____
_____
_____
_____
_____
_____
_____
_____
_____

I'M PRAYING FOR: _____

_____
_____
_____
_____
_____

I'M THANKFUL FOR: _____

_____
_____
_____
_____
_____

TODAY'S DATE:

TODAY'S VERSE: _____

_____
_____
_____
_____
_____
_____
_____
_____
_____
_____
_____
_____
_____
_____
_____

HOW IT APPLIES TO MY LIFE:

_____
_____
_____
_____
_____
_____
_____
_____
_____
_____
_____
_____
_____
_____
_____

I'M PRAYING FOR: _____

_____
_____
_____
_____
_____

I'M THANKFUL FOR: _____

_____
_____
_____
_____
_____

TODAY'S DATE:

TODAY'S VERSE: _____

_____
_____
_____
_____
_____
_____
_____
_____
_____
_____
_____

HOW IT APPLIES TO MY LIFE:

_____
_____
_____
_____
_____
_____
_____
_____
_____
_____
_____

I'M PRAYING FOR: _____

_____
_____
_____
_____
_____

I'M THANKFUL FOR: _____

_____
_____
_____
_____

TODAY'S DATE:

TODAY'S VERSE: _____

_____
_____
_____
_____
_____
_____
_____
_____
_____
_____
_____
_____
_____
_____

HOW IT APPLIES TO MY LIFE:

_____
_____
_____
_____
_____
_____
_____
_____
_____
_____
_____
_____

I'M PRAYING FOR: _____

_____
_____
_____
_____
_____
_____

I'M THANKFUL FOR: _____

_____
_____
_____
_____
_____
_____

TODAY'S DATE:

TODAY'S VERSE: _____

_____
_____
_____
_____
_____
_____
_____
_____
_____
_____

HOW IT APPLIES TO MY LIFE:

_____
_____
_____
_____
_____
_____
_____
_____
_____
_____
_____

I'M PRAYING FOR: _____

_____
_____
_____
_____

I'M THANKFUL FOR: _____

_____
_____
_____
_____
_____

TODAY'S DATE:

TODAY'S VERSE: _____

_____
_____
_____
_____
_____
_____
_____
_____
_____
_____
_____
_____
_____

HOW IT APPLIES TO MY LIFE:

_____
_____
_____
_____
_____
_____
_____
_____
_____
_____
_____
_____

I'M PRAYING FOR: _____

_____
_____
_____
_____
_____

I'M THANKFUL FOR: _____

_____
_____
_____
_____

TODAY'S DATE:

TODAY'S VERSE: _____

HOW IT APPLIES TO MY LIFE:

I'M PRAYING FOR: _____

I'M THANKFUL FOR: _____

TODAY'S DATE:

TODAY'S VERSE: _____

_____
_____
_____
_____
_____
_____
_____
_____
_____
_____
_____
_____
_____

HOW IT APPLIES TO MY LIFE:

_____
_____
_____
_____
_____
_____
_____
_____
_____
_____
_____
_____
_____
_____
_____
_____

I'M PRAYING FOR: _____

_____
_____
_____
_____
_____
_____
_____

I'M THANKFUL FOR: _____

_____
_____
_____
_____
_____
_____

TODAY'S DATE:

TODAY'S VERSE: _____

HOW IT APPLIES TO MY LIFE:

I'M PRAYING FOR: _____

I'M THANKFUL FOR: _____

TODAY'S DATE:

TODAY'S VERSE: _____

_____
_____
_____
_____
_____
_____
_____
_____
_____
_____
_____
_____
_____

HOW IT APPLIES TO MY LIFE:

_____
_____
_____
_____
_____
_____
_____
_____
_____
_____
_____
_____

I'M PRAYING FOR: _____

_____
_____
_____
_____
_____

I'M THANKFUL FOR: _____

_____
_____
_____
_____
_____

TODAY'S DATE:

TODAY'S VERSE: _____

_____
_____
_____
_____
_____
_____
_____
_____
_____
_____
_____
_____

HOW IT APPLIES TO MY LIFE:

_____
_____
_____
_____
_____
_____
_____
_____
_____
_____
_____
_____

I'M PRAYING FOR: _____

_____
_____
_____
_____
_____
_____

I'M THANKFUL FOR: _____

_____
_____
_____
_____
_____

TODAY'S DATE:

TODAY'S VERSE: _____

_____
_____
_____
_____
_____
_____
_____
_____
_____
_____
_____
_____

HOW IT APPLIES TO MY LIFE:

_____
_____
_____
_____
_____
_____
_____
_____
_____
_____
_____

I'M PRAYING FOR: _____

_____
_____
_____
_____
_____
_____

I'M THANKFUL FOR: _____

_____
_____
_____
_____
_____
_____

TODAY'S DATE:

TODAY'S VERSE: _____

_____
_____
_____
_____
_____
_____
_____
_____
_____
_____
_____
_____
_____
_____

HOW IT APPLIES TO MY LIFE:

_____
_____
_____
_____
_____
_____
_____
_____
_____
_____
_____
_____
_____
_____

I'M PRAYING FOR: _____

_____
_____
_____
_____
_____

I'M THANKFUL FOR: _____

_____
_____
_____
_____
_____
_____

TODAY'S DATE:

TODAY'S VERSE: _____

_____
_____
_____
_____
_____
_____
_____
_____
_____
_____
_____
_____
_____
_____
_____

HOW IT APPLIES TO MY LIFE:

_____
_____
_____
_____
_____
_____
_____
_____
_____
_____
_____
_____
_____

I'M PRAYING FOR: _____

_____
_____
_____
_____
_____

I'M THANKFUL FOR: _____

_____
_____
_____
_____
_____

TODAY'S DATE:

TODAY'S VERSE: _____

_____
_____
_____
_____
_____
_____
_____
_____
_____
_____

HOW IT APPLIES TO MY LIFE:

_____
_____
_____
_____
_____
_____
_____
_____
_____
_____

I'M PRAYING FOR: _____

_____
_____
_____
_____
_____

I'M THANKFUL FOR: _____

_____
_____
_____
_____
_____

TODAY'S DATE:

TODAY'S VERSE: _____

_____
_____
_____
_____
_____
_____
_____
_____
_____
_____
_____
_____
_____
_____
_____

HOW IT APPLIES TO MY LIFE:

_____
_____
_____
_____
_____
_____
_____
_____
_____
_____
_____
_____
_____
_____

I'M PRAYING FOR: _____

_____
_____
_____
_____
_____

I'M THANKFUL FOR: _____

_____
_____
_____
_____
_____

TODAY'S DATE:

TODAY'S VERSE: _____

_____
_____
_____
_____
_____
_____
_____
_____
_____
_____
_____
_____

HOW IT APPLIES TO MY LIFE:

_____
_____
_____
_____
_____
_____
_____
_____
_____
_____
_____
_____
_____
_____

I'M PRAYING FOR: _____

_____
_____
_____
_____
_____

I'M THANKFUL FOR: _____

_____
_____
_____
_____
_____

TODAY'S DATE:

TODAY'S VERSE: _____

_____
_____
_____
_____
_____
_____
_____
_____
_____
_____
_____
_____
_____
_____

HOW IT APPLIES TO MY LIFE:

_____
_____
_____
_____
_____
_____
_____
_____
_____
_____
_____
_____
_____

I'M PRAYING FOR: _____

_____
_____
_____
_____
_____

I'M THANKFUL FOR: _____

_____
_____
_____
_____
_____

TODAY'S DATE:

TODAY'S VERSE: _____

_____
_____
_____
_____
_____
_____
_____
_____
_____
_____
_____

HOW IT APPLIES TO MY LIFE:

_____
_____
_____
_____
_____
_____
_____
_____
_____
_____
_____
_____

I'M PRAYING FOR: _____

_____
_____
_____
_____
_____

I'M THANKFUL FOR: _____

_____
_____
_____
_____

TODAY'S DATE:

TODAY'S VERSE: _____
_____
_____
_____
_____
_____
_____
_____
_____
_____
_____
_____
_____

HOW IT APPLIES TO MY LIFE:
_____
_____
_____
_____
_____
_____
_____
_____
_____
_____
_____
_____

I'M PRAYING FOR: _____
_____
_____
_____
_____
_____

I'M THANKFUL FOR: _____
_____
_____
_____
_____
_____

TODAY'S DATE:

TODAY'S VERSE: _____

_____
_____
_____
_____
_____
_____
_____
_____
_____
_____
_____
_____

HOW IT APPLIES TO MY LIFE:

_____
_____
_____
_____
_____
_____
_____
_____
_____
_____
_____
_____
_____
_____

I'M PRAYING FOR: _____

_____
_____
_____
_____
_____

I'M THANKFUL FOR: _____

_____
_____
_____
_____
_____

TODAY'S DATE:

TODAY'S VERSE: _____
_____
_____
_____
_____
_____
_____
_____
_____
_____
_____
_____
_____
_____
_____
_____
_____

HOW IT APPLIES TO MY LIFE:
_____
_____
_____
_____
_____
_____
_____
_____
_____
_____
_____
_____

I'M PRAYING FOR: _____
_____
_____
_____
_____
_____

I'M THANKFUL FOR: _____
_____
_____
_____
_____
_____

TODAY'S DATE:

TODAY'S VERSE: _____

_____
_____
_____
_____
_____
_____
_____
_____
_____
_____

HOW IT APPLIES TO MY LIFE:

_____
_____
_____
_____
_____
_____
_____
_____
_____
_____
_____

I'M PRAYING FOR: _____

_____
_____
_____
_____
_____

I'M THANKFUL FOR: _____

_____
_____
_____
_____
_____

TODAY'S DATE: _____

TODAY'S VERSE: _____
_____
_____
_____
_____
_____
_____
_____
_____
_____
_____
_____
_____
_____

HOW IT APPLIES TO MY LIFE:
_____
_____
_____
_____
_____
_____
_____
_____
_____
_____
_____
_____
_____

I'M PRAYING FOR: _____
_____
_____
_____
_____
_____

I'M THANKFUL FOR: _____
_____
_____
_____
_____
_____

TODAY'S DATE:

TODAY'S VERSE: _____

_____
_____
_____
_____
_____
_____
_____
_____
_____
_____
_____
_____
_____
_____

HOW IT APPLIES TO MY LIFE:

_____
_____
_____
_____
_____
_____
_____
_____
_____
_____
_____
_____
_____
_____
_____

I'M PRAYING FOR: _____

_____
_____
_____
_____
_____

I'M THANKFUL FOR: _____

_____
_____
_____
_____
_____

Made in the USA
Monee, IL
06 September 2022

13378463R00063